INDIA

WORLD ADVENTURES

BY HARRIET BRUNDLE

BookLife

©This edition was
published in 2018. First
published in 2016.

Book Life
King's Lynn
Norfolk PE30 4LS

ISBN: 978-1-910512-65-4

Written by:
Harriet Brundle
Edited by:
Gemma McMullen
Designed by:
Matt Rumbelow

A catalogue record for this book
is available from the British Library.

INDIA
WORLD ADVENTURES

CONTENTS

Words in **bold** can be found in the glossary on page 24.

WHERE IS INDIA?

India is a large country in the southern part of Asia. India is between China and Pakistan.

PAKISTAN

CHINA

INDIA

India has a very large **population**. Only one country in the world (China) has more people living in it than India.

WEATHER AND LANDSCAPE

The weather in India is mostly very hot. The temperature is highest between March and June.

India has lots of different landscapes. Some parts of the country have mountains and other parts are next to the sea.

CLOTHING

A **traditional** style of clothing for ladies in India is a sari. The sari is usually wrapped around the waist and over the shoulder.

SARI

TURBAN

Indian men usually only wear their traditional clothing for special **occasions**.

For some Indian men, part of their traditional dress is a long piece of material wrapped around the head. This is called a turban.

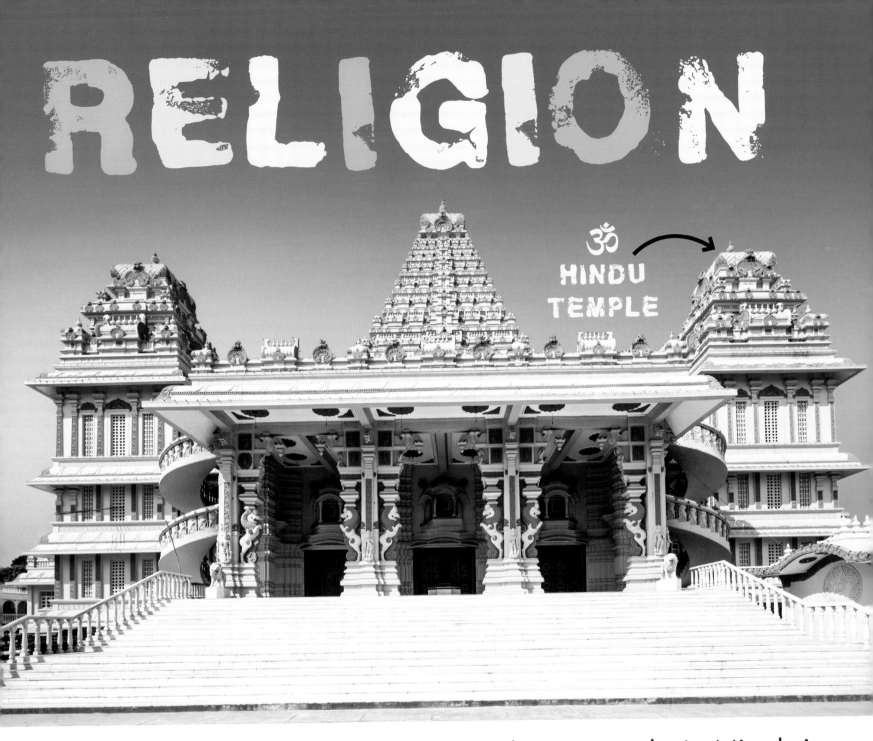

RELIGION

HINDU TEMPLE

The religion followed by most Indian people is Hinduism.
Many different religions are also celebrated
in India including Christianity, Sikhism and Buddhism.

Hindus celebrate the Festival of Lights, known as Diwali. When Diwali is celebrated, candles are lit, gifts are given and families eat together.

FOOD

The dish thought to be most popular in India is curry. Indian food is known for having lots of different herbs and spices.

Food such as bread is traditionally eaten
using just the right hand. The bread is torn
into pieces and used to scoop food like a spoon.

AT SCHOOL

Children in India must go to school until they are 14 years old. Indian children are taught subjects such as maths, sports and how to read and write English.

VILLAGE

CITY

There are fewer schools in the villages compared
to the number of schools in the cities.

AT HOME

The types of houses in the cities are very different to those in the villages. The capital of India, New Delhi, has sky scrapers and **modern** houses.

In the villages the homes are usually made from clay and straw. Lots of the homes do not have electricity.

FAMILIES

Indian families traditionally live in the same house. Grandparents, parents, aunts, uncles and children all live together.

Traditionally men in the family must go out to work and ladies must look after the home and children.

SPORT

The most popular sport in India is cricket. The Indian Premier League for cricket is held in India every year.

THE INDIAN
HOCKEY TEAM
HAVE WON
OLYMPIC GOLD
MEDALS!

Lots of other sports are also popular in India, including football and hockey.

FUN FACTS

India is home to the largest population of Bengal tigers in the world.

Bollywood is the Indian film industry. Bollywood makes over 1,000 films every year.

GLOSSARY

modern: something that has been made using recent ideas

occasions: special events

population: amount of people living in that place

traditional: ways of behaving that have been done for a long time

INDEX

Photocredits: Abbreviations: l-left, r-right, b-bottom, t-top, c-centre, m-middle.
All images are courtesy of Shutterstock.com.

Front Cover, 24 – Jay Venkat. 1 – Aleksey Klints. 2 – Nila Newsom. 3, 8 – Ami Parikh. 5 – Radiokafka. 6, 10 – saiko3p. 7t – Dchauy. 7b – Lena Serditova. 9 – stockyimages. 11 – wong yu liang. 12br – Dinesh Picholiya. 12tr, 12bl – HLPhoto. 13 – szefei. 13inset – Simone van den Berg. 14 – steve estvanik. 15t – Ailisa. 15b – Lena Serditova. 16 – Kunal Mehta. 17 – NOWAK LUKASZ. 18 – Monkey Business Images. 19 – Dragon Images. 19inset – Rehan Qureshi. 20 – Rosli Othman. 21 – Maksym Gorpenyuk. 21inset – Kostsov. 22 – KAMONRAT. 23 – Raphael Christinat.
All facts, statistics, web addresses and URLs in this book were verified as valid and accurate at time of writing. No responsibility for any changes to external websites or references can be accepted by either the author or publisher.